Quick
Easy

igloo

Published by Igloo Books Ltd
Cottage Farm
Sywell
NN6 0BJ
www.igloo-books.com

10 9 8 7 6 5 4 3 2 1

ISBN: 978 1 84852 722 5

Project Managed by R&R Publications Marketing Pty Ltd

Food Photography: R&R Photostudio (www.rrphotostudio.com.au)
Recipe Development: R&R Test Kitchen

Front cover photograph © Getty Images/John E. Kelly

Printed in and manufactured in China

Contents

Coconut, Sweet Potato, and Spinach Soup

Preparation 10 mins **Cooking** 25 mins **Calories** 289

2 tbsps butter

455g (1lb) sweet potatoes, cut into 1cm (⅓in) dice

1 onion, chopped

2 cloves garlic, crushed

1 tsp grated root ginger

1 tbsp medium curry paste

2½ cups vegetable stock

1 cup coconut milk

juice of 1 lime

½ tsp dried crushed chilies

3 cups fresh spinach, shredded

salt and black peppers

1 Melt the butter in a saucepan and fry the sweet potatoes, onion, garlic, ginger and curry paste for 5 minutes or until lightly golden.

2 Add the stock, coconut milk, lime juice and chili. Bring to the boil, cover and simmer for 15 minutes or until the sweet potatoes are tender.

3 Leave the soup to cool a little, then purée half of it with a hand blender. Return the purée to the pan, add the spinach and cook for 1–2 minutes, until the spinach has just wilted and the soup has heated through. Season to taste.

Serves 4

Note: Sweet potatoes have a slightly nutty flavor. They also make the texture of this soup really creamy. For a fantastic light meal, serve the soup with naan bread.

Lemon and Herb Basted Scallops

Preparation 10 mins **Cooking** 5 mins **Calories** 125

4 tbsps butter, melted
2 tbsps lemon juice
1 clove garlic, crushed
1 tsp basil, finely chopped
1 tsp cilantro, finely chopped
1 tsp mint, finely chopped
500g (18oz) package frozen scallops
1 red onion, cut into wedges
1 red capsicum, cut into triangles
watercress and lemon wedges to garnish

1 Combine the butter, lemon juice, garlic and herbs and set aside.

2 Thread scallops, onion and capsicum onto skewers and brush with the butter mixture.

3 Place the skewers onto a preheated broiler plate turning once and brushing with butter mixture, until scallops are just cooked (approximately 5 minutes).

4 Serve garnished with watercress and lemon wedges.

Serves 6

Variation: Exchange the scallops for fresh peeled shrimp.

Cheese and Herb Salad

Preparation 10 mins **Calories** 120

500g (18oz) baked ricotta cheese, chopped

2 tomatoes, cut into wedges

90g (3oz) marinated olives

440g (1lb) canned artichoke hearts, drained and quartered

375g (13oz) assorted lettuce leaves

4 tbsps mixed fresh herb leaves, such as cilantro, parsley, sage and chives

3 tbsps balsamic or red-wine vinegar

185g (6oz) croûtons

1 Arrange ricotta cheese, tomatoes, olives, artichoke hearts, lettuce leaves and herbs on a serving platter. Sprinkle with vinegar, scatter with croûtons and serve immediately.

Serves 4

Serving suggestion: Italian breadstalks make an interesting accompaniment to this Italian-inspired salad.

Note: Baked ricotta cheese is available from Italian food stores and good cheese shops. If it is unavailable feta cheese is a good alternative.

Greek Salad

Preparation 10 mins **Calories** 360

1 lettuce, leaves separated and shredded

2 tomatoes, sliced

1 small cucumber, sliced

1 red capsicum, cut into thin slices

1 small onion, thinly sliced

1 cup feta cheese, cut into small cubes

12 black olives

Lemon and Mint Dressing
6 tbsps olive oil
2 tbsps lemon juice
2 tsps chopped fresh mint
2 tsps chopped fresh marjoram
salt and black pepper

1 Line a large serving platter or salad bowl with the lettuce. Top with the tomatoes, cucumber, capsicum, onion, feta and olives.

2 To make the dressing, place oil, lemon juice, mint and marjoram in a screwtop jar and season to taste. Shake well. Spoon over the salad. Serve immediately.

Serves 4

Carrot and Sweet Potato Soup

Preparation 10 mins **Cooking** 40 mins **Calories** 276

2 tbsp butter
1 large onion, chopped
3 large carrots, chopped
1 large sweet potato, chopped
4 cups chicken or vegetable stock
¾ cup sour cream
2 tbsps chopped fresh dill

1 Melt the butter in a saucepan over a medium heat. Add the onion, carrots and sweet potato. Cook for 5 minutes.

2 Stir in the stock. Bring to the boil. Simmer for 30 minutes. Cool slightly.

3 Purée the soup. Return the soup to a clean saucepan. Stir in the sour cream. Cook, without boiling, stirring constantly, for 5 minutes or until the soup is hot. Stir in the dill. Serve immediately.

Serves 4

Variation: Exchange the carrots for 3 large red capsicums.

Chicken and Corn Chowder

Preparation 10 mins **Cooking** 30 mins **Calories** 320

1 tbsp vegetable oil
1 small onion, diced
255g (9oz) boneless chicken breast fillets, shredded
3 potatoes, chopped
3 cups chicken stock
1½ cups canned corn kernels, drained and chopped
1¼ cups milk
1 bay leaf
freshly ground black pepper
1 tbsp lemon juice
2 tbsps fresh parsley, chopped
1 tbsp snipped fresh chives
½ cup shredded Parmesan cheese

1 Heat the oil in a saucepan over a medium heat, add the onion and cook, stirring, for 4–5 minutes or until the onion is soft. Add the chicken and cook for 2 minutes longer or until the chicken just changes color.

2 Add the potatoes and stock and bring to the boil. Reduce the heat and simmer for 10 minutes or until the potatoes are almost cooked. Stir the corn, milk, bay leaf and pepper to taste into the stock mixture and bring to a boil. Reduce the heat and simmer for 3–4 minutes or until the potatoes are cooked. Remove the bay leaf. Stir in the lemon juice, parsley, chives and pepper to taste. Just prior to serving, sprinkle with the Parmesan.

Serves 6

Note: To chop the corn, place in a blender and process using the pulse button until the corn is coarsely chopped. Creamed sweetcorn can be used in place of the kernels if you wish. If using creamed corn there's no need to chop it.

Gnocchi with Mascarpone and Blue Cheese

Preparation 5 mins **Cooking** 10 mins **Calories** 460

400g (14oz) fresh gnocchi

1 tbsp pine nuts

½ cup mascarpone cheese

1 cup gorgonzola cheese, crumbled

salt and black pepper

1 Cook the gnocchi according to the packet instructions. Drain well, then transfer to a shallow flameproof dish.

2 Preheat the broiler to high. Place the pine nuts in the broiler pan and toast for 2–3 minutes, stirring from time to time, until golden. Keep an eye on them, as they can burn quickly.

3 Meanwhile, put the mascarpone and gorgonzola in a saucepan and warm over a very low heat, stirring, until melted. Season to taste. Spoon over the gnocchi, then broiler for 2–3 minutes, until bubbling and golden. Scatter with the pine nuts and serve.

Serves 4

Note: Creamy mascarpone and gorgonzola produce this meltingly good Italian gnocchi dish. It's ideal served with a lightly dressed green or mixed salad.

Tomato and Mozzarella Salad

Preparation 10 mins **Cooking** 5 mins **Calories** 306

6 plum tomatoes, sliced

1 cup mozzarella cheese, drained and sliced

2 scallions, sliced

6 tbsps black olives

salt and black pepper

Dressing

3 tbsps extra virgin olive oil

1 clove garlic, crushed

2 tsps balsamic vinegar

2 tbsps chopped fresh basil

1 Arrange the tomatoes, mozzarella, scallions and olives in layers on serving plates and season to taste.

2 To make the dressing, heat the oil and garlic in a small saucepan over a very low heat for 2 minutes or until the garlic has softened but not browned. Remove the pan from the heat, add the vinegar and basil, stir well then pour over the salad and serve.

Serves 4

Note: This classic Italian salad never fails to please and the hot dressing works really well with it. Don't skimp on the fresh basil or balsamic vinegar – it won't be the same.

Caesar Salad with Crispy Prosciutto

Preparation 15 mins **Cooking** 15 mins **Calories** 313

4 slices day-old bread, cut into 1cm cubes

4 large slices prosciutto

2 lettuce cos, torn into bite-sized pieces

½ cup Parmesan cheese, shredded, plus extra to serve (optional)

Dressing

8 anchovies, drained and mashed

2 tbsp extra virgin olive oil

3 tbsps mayonnaise

1 clove garlic, crushed

1 tsp white-wine vinegar

½ tsp Worcestershire sauce

freshly ground black pepper

1 Preheat the oven to 200°C (400°F). To make the croûtons, place the bread cubes on a baking tray and cook for 10–12 minutes, turning occasionally, until crisp and golden.

2 Preheat the broiler to high. Broil the prosciutto for 1 minute or until very crisp, then leave to cool for 2 minutes. Place the lettuce leaves, croûtons and Parmesan in a bowl.

3 To make the dressing, put the anchovies, oil, mayonnaise, garlic, vinegar, Worcestershire sauce and pepper into a bowl and beat until smooth. Spoon over the lettuce and croûtons, then toss until well coated. Top with the crispy prosciutto and extra Parmesan (if using) and serve.

Serves 4

Note: Even the classic Caesar salad can be improved upon. Here, broilered prosciutto adds extra crunch and a dash of Worcestershire sauce peps up the traditional dressing.

Vine Tomatoes and Goat's Cheese Bruschetta

Preparation 10 mins **Cooking** 20 mins **Calories** 278

455g (1lb) small vine-ripened tomatoes

2 tbsps extra virgin olive oil

1 clove garlic, crushed

4 sprigs fresh thyme

4 thick slices ciabatta bread, cut diagonally

4 tbsps ready-made tapenade

½ cup soft goat's cheese, cut into chunks

fresh basil leaves to garnish

1 Preheat the oven to 220°C (400°F). Place the tomatoes, still on the vine, in a roasting tin and drizzle over the oil. Scatter over the garlic and thyme sprigs. Roast for 15 minutes or until the tomatoes are tender. Divide the tomatoes into 4 portions roughly equal, each still attached to part of the vine.

2 Meanwhile, preheat the broiler to high. Toast the bread on both sides until golden. Spread each slice with 1 tablespoon of tapenade, add a few chunks of goat's cheese and top with the tomatoes on the vine. Drizzle over the juices from the roasting tin, sprinkle with the basil leaves and serve.

Serves 4

Note: The tapenade in this dish is full of strong Mediterranean flavors – capers, anchovies and olives. You can use loose cherry tomatoes, but cook them for a few minutes less.

Lamb with Mint Butter and Saffron Mash

Preparation 15 mins **Cooking** 25 mins **Calories** 808

910g (2lb) floury potatoes cut into chunks

salt and black pepper

2 tbsps butter, softened

2 tbsps chopped fresh mint, plus extra leaves to garnish

½ tsp ground cumin

4 tbsps light cream

pinch of saffron strands

4 lamb leg steaks

1 Cook the potatoes in a large saucepan of lightly salted water for 15 minutes or until tender. Meanwhile, mash together half the butter with the mint, cumin and a little pepper, then cover and refrigerate. Put the cream and saffron in a small pan, gently heat through, then remove from the heat and let stand for 5 minutes to infuse.

2 Preheat the broiler to high. Season the lamb steaks and broil for 4–5 minutes each side, or until done to your liking. Cover with aluminum foil and leave to rest for 5 minutes. Meanwhile, drain the potatoes well and mash with a potato masher, then mix in the remaining butter and the saffron cream and season.

3 Divide the chilled mint butter between the steaks and broiler for a few seconds until it melts. Serve the steaks with the saffron mash and pan juices. Garnish with the mint.

Serves 4

Note: Creamy saffron mash and mint butter turn juicy lamb steaks into a wonderful meal. Serve this dish with some fresh green vegetables.

Spiced Pork with Hummus and Cilantro Oil

Preparation 15 mins **Cooking** 15 mins **Calories** 548

4 pork fillets, about 225g (9oz) each
1 tbsp olive oil
1 tsp paprika
½ tsp cayenne pepper
290g (10oz) of fresh hummus
lemon wedges to serve
cilantro leaves to garnish

Cilantro Oil

4 tbsps extra virgin olive oil
2 scallions, finely chopped
1 tbsp chopped cilantro leaves
salt and black pepper

1 Preheat the oven to 180°C (350°F). Wipe the pork with damp absorbent paper. Mix the oil with the paprika and cayenne pepper. Rub over the pork fillets.

2 Heat a heavy-based skillet, add the pork and fry for 2 minutes, turning, until seared all over. Add 2 tablespoons of water, cover and simmer for 10 minutes. Remove from the heat and let stand for 5 minutes. Put the hummus into a baking dish and place in the oven for 10 minutes to heat through.

3 Meanwhile, make the cilantro oil. Heat the oil in a small pan, add the scallions and cilantro and cook for 3–4 minutes, until the scallions have softened. Cool slightly, season, then blend until fairly smooth in a blender. Serve the pork in slices with the hummus, cilantro oil and lemon wedges. Garnish with the cilantro.

Serves 4

Note: The sunny flavors of the Mediterranean have inspired this pork dish. It's good served with pita bread.

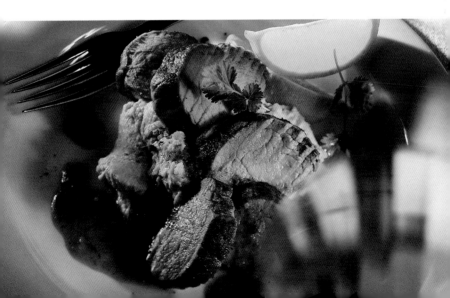

Honeyed Gammon with Pineapple Salsa

Preparation 15 mins **Cooking** 10 mins **Calories** 535

4 thick smoked ham steaks, about 225g (9oz) each

2 sprigs fresh thyme

1 tbsp clear honey

lime wedges to serve

cilantro leaves to garnish

Salsa

2 tomatoes

225g (9oz) pineapple, cut into 1cm (⅓in) cubes

1 clove garlic, crushed

1 red chili, deseeded and chopped

2 tbsps extra virgin olive oil

juice of ½ lime

2 tbsps chopped cilantro leaves

salt and black pepper

1 First make the salsa. Put the tomatoes in a bowl and cover with boiling water. Leave for 30 seconds, then skin, deseed and dice. Combine with the pineapple, garlic, chili, oil, lime juice and cilantro. Season to taste and set aside.

2 Preheat the broiler to high. Score the fat around the edge of each steak and rub all over with the thyme sprigs. Brush with honey and broil the ham for 2–3 minutes each side, until tender and cooked through. Serve with the salsa and lime wedges and garnish with the cilantro.

Serves 4

Note: This is not the usual version of ham and pineapple! A spicy pineapple salsa really sets the steaks alight. Serve with either rice or potatoes and a fresh green salad.

Beef Fillet with Wild Mushrooms

Preparation 25 mins **Cooking** 20 mins **Calories** 436

15g (½ oz) dried porcini mushrooms

6 tbsps butter

4 beef fillet steaks

3 cups mixed fresh wild mushrooms, sliced

1 clove garlic, crushed

1 tsp chopped fresh thyme, plus extra to garnish

½ cup red wine

½ cup beef stock

salt and black pepper

1 Preheat the oven to 160°C (325°). Cover the dried mushrooms with 85ml (3fl oz) of boiling water. Soak for 15 minutes or until softened. Strain, reserving the soaking liquid, then chop the mushrooms. Melt half a tablespoon of the butter and fry the steaks for 2–3 minutes each side, until browned. Wrap loosely in aluminum foil and keep warm in the oven.

2 Add half a tablespoon of the butter to the pan and fry the fresh mushrooms, dried mushrooms, garlic and thyme for 4 minutes or until the fresh mushrooms have softened. Add the wine, increase the heat and boil for 1–2 minutes, until the sauce has reduced by half.

3 Mix the dried mushroom soaking liquid with the beef stock, then add to the pan and simmer for 3 minutes. Stir in the remaining butter and season. Serve with the steaks, garnished with the thyme.

Serves 4

Note: Fillet steak, red wine and mushrooms is a much-loved combination. Here, both dried and fresh mushrooms are used to give the sauce an intense flavor.

Chicken Parcels with Tarragon Cream Sauce

Preparation 10 mins **Cooking** 35 mins **Calories** 545

4 large skinless boneless chicken breasts

8 sun-dried tomatoes in oil, drained

8 slices rindless smoked bacon

2 tbsps olive oil

455g (1lb) baby leeks

1½ cups fresh chicken stock

2 tbsps brandy

⅔ cup light cream

2 tbsps chopped fresh tarragon, plus extra to garnish

salt and black pepper

1 Preheat the oven to 200°C (400°F). Cut a deep slice into 1 side of each chicken breast to make a pocket. Place 2 tomatoes in each pocket, then wrap 2 bacon slices around each breast. Secure with wetted cocktail stalks.

2 Heat 1 tablespoon of the oil in an ovenproof skillet. Cook the chicken for 2–3 minutes, turning once, until browned all over. Transfer to the oven and cook for 15 minutes or until the chicken is cooked through. Transfer to a plate, remove the cocktail stalks and keep warm. Meanwhile, preheat the broiler to high. Brush the leeks with the remaining oil and broil for 6–8 minutes, until softened.

3 Meanwhile, add the stock and brandy to the skillet. Cook over a high heat for 3 minutes, stirring and scraping, until reduced by half. Beat in the cream and tarragon and simmer for 2–3 minutes, until slightly thickened. Season, then spoon over the chicken parcels and leeks. Garnish with the reserved tarragon.

Serves 4

Note: It's a surprise when you cut into these chicken breasts and discover a delicious filling of sun-dried tomatoes. The rich sauce and baby leeks are perfect accompaniments.

Balsamic Duck Breasts with Potato Rösti

Preparation 10 mins **Cooking** 25 mins **Calories** 460

2 tbsps balsamic vinegar
1 tsp clear honey
1 clove garlic, crushed
pinch of five-spice powder
salt and black pepper
4 boneless duck breasts,
about 170g (6oz) each
455g (1lb) waxy potatoes,
peeled and shredded
2 tbsps butter
2 tbsps olive oil
4 tbsps apple and plum
chutney to serve
fresh herbs, such as marjoram
or basil, to garnish

1 Combine the vinegar, honey, garlic, five-spice powder, salt and pepper in a bowl. Cut several slashes in each duck breast with a sharp knife and rub in the mixture. Set aside.

2 Rinse the potatoes, squeeze dry in a clean dish towel, then season. Heat the butter and the oil in a skillet, add 4 tablespoons of the potato mixture (about half) and press down gently to make 4 rösti (potato cakes). Fry for 5–6 minutes each side, until browned and cooked through. Repeat to make 4 more.

3 Meanwhile, preheat the broiler to high. Cook the duck close to the heat for 3–4 minutes each side, until charred. Wrap in aluminum foil and leave to rest for 5 minutes, then slice it and serve with any juices, the rösti, and spoonfuls of the chutney. Garnish with the fresh herbs.

Serves 4

Note: The sweet-and-sour apple and plum chutney cuts through the richness of the duck, and the crispy potato pancakes help to bring all the intense flavors together.

Variation: Exchange half the potato for sweet potato and prepare the rösti the same way.

Quick Sausage Sizzle

Preparation 6 mins **Cooking** 12 mins **Calories** 900

1.8 kg (4lb) pork or beef sausages

910g (1lb) onions, thinly sliced

3 tbsps olive oil

Honey and Chili Marinade

¼ cup red wine

½ cup honey

¼ tsp ground chili

1 To make the marinade, mix all the ingredients together.

2 Place the sausages in a large saucepan and cover with cold water. Heat slowly until simmering point is reached, then simmer for 5 minutes. Drain well. Refrigerate until needed.

3 Heat the barbecue until hot and grease the grill bars with oil. Pour the honey and chili marinade into a heatproof bowl and place at the side of the barbecue. Arrange the sausages from left to right on the grill or hotplate and brush with the marinade. Turn and brush with marinade after 1 minute and continue turning and basting for 10 minutes until the sausages are well glazed and cooked through. Give a final brushing with the marinade remove them to a serving platter.

4 Oil the hot plate and place on the onions. Toss at intervals and drizzle with a little oil as they cook. Serve the sausages with the onions and accompany with salad and garlic bread.

Serves 4

Note: This method is suitable for cooking a large number of sausages to serve around. Pork or beef thick sausages are used, which are simmered in water before placing on the barbecue. This prevents them from splitting and reduces cooking time. Calculate the number of sausages you need for the number of people to be served.

Lamb Noisettes with Mustard and Rosemary

Preparation 5 mins **Cooking** 10 mins **Calories** 140

4 tbsps wholegrain mustard

2 tbsps finely chopped rosemary leaves

½ tsp minced garlic

4 lamb noisettes

1 Combine mustard, rosemary leaves and garlic. Spread mustard mixture over both sides of the noisettes. Place under a preheated broiler and cook for 5 minutes each side or until cooked as desired.

Serves 4

Serving suggestion: Crusty bread with boiled or steamed baby carrots and broccoli are easy accompaniments for this tasty main meal.

Note: A noisette is a small round steak, usually of lamb. The word means 'hazelnut' in French, signifying the roundness and meatiness of the particular cut. Because the cut is so tender, it cooks very quickly.

Cajun Chops

Preparation 10 mins **Cooking** 18 mins **Calories** 696

6 tbsps butter

3 tsps Cajun seasoning

1 small red chili, seeded and chopped

12 lamb chops

1 tbsp olive oil

1 Beat the butter to soften it and mix in 1½ teaspoons of the Cajun seasoning and all the chili. Place the butter along the center of a piece of plastic wrap or greaseproof paper to 1cm (⅓in) thickness. Fold the plastic wrap over the butter then roll it up. Smooth into a sausage shape and twist the ends. Refrigerate to firm.

2 Trim the chops if necessary and snip the membrane at the side to prevent curling. Flatten them slightly with the side of a meat mallet. Mix the remaining Cajun seasoning with the olive oil then rub the mixture well into both sides of the chops. Place them in a single layer onto a tray, cover and let stand for 20 minutes at room temperature, or longer in the refrigerator.

3 Heat the barbecue or electric broiler to high. Place a sheet of baking paper on the grill bars, making a few slashes between the bars for ventilation. Place the chops on the broiler and cook for 3 minutes each side for medium or 4 minutes for well-done. When cooked, transfer to a serving plate and top each chop with a round slice of Cajun butter.

Serves 3–4

Teriyaki Chicken

Preparation 5 mins **Cooking** 5 mins **Calories** 181

455g (1lb) chicken skinless fillets

Teriyaki Marinade
½ cup soy sauce
2 tbsps brown sugar
½ tsp minced ginger
2 tbsps wine vinegar
1 clove garlic, crushed
2 tbsps tomato sauce

1 To make the marinade, mix all the ingredients together.

2 Place the fillets in a non-metallic container and stir in about half a cup of teriyaki marinade. Cover and marinate for 30 minutes at room temperature or place in the refrigerator for several hours or overnight.

3 Heat the barbecue until hot. Place a sheet of baking paper over the broiler bars and make a few slits between the bars for ventilation, or place baking paper on the hot plate. Place the tenderloins on broiler and cook for 2 minutes each side until cooked through and golden, brushing with marinade as they cook.

Serves 2–4

Serving Suggestions

A Serve with steamed rice and vegetables.

B Toss into salad greens to make a hot salad. Dress the salad with 1 tablespoon of teriyaki marinade, 1 tablespoon of vinegar and 3 tablespoons of salad oil.

C Stuff into heated pocket breads along with shredded lettuce, cucumber and onion rings and drizzle with an extra spoonful of the teriyaki marinade.

Hot Dogs with Mustard, Relish and Pickles

Preparation 1 min **Cooking** 12 mins **Calories** 370

12 frankfurters or thin
sausages

1 cup barbecue sauce

12 hot-dog rolls

mild mustard for serving

gherkin relish or tomato pickles
to serve

1 Heat the barbecue and oil the grill bars. Place the frankfurters or sausages and turn to heat on the grill evenly, so the skin doesn't burst. Cook for 10–12 minutes, brushing with a little barbecue sauce as they're turned. Turn down the heat or push them to a cooler part of the barbecue if they cook too quickly.

2 Split the rolls, keeping the 2 halves attached and place the cut side down on the hot plate to toast.

3 Fill each roll with a frankfurter or sausage, squeeze a row of mustard along the side and spoon in the gherkin relish or tomato pickles.

Makes 12

Perfect T-Bone Steak

Preparation 20 mins **Cooking** 5–15 mins **Calories** 344

4 T-bone steaks
2 tsps garlic crushed
2 tsp oil
salt and black pepper

Garlic Butter
4 tbsp butter
1 tsp crushed garlic
1 tbsp parsley, chopped
2 tsps lemon juice

1 Bring the steaks to room temperature. Mix the garlic, oil, salt and pepper together. Rub onto both sides of the steak. Stand for 10–15 minutes at room temperature.

2 Heat the barbecue until hot and oil the grill bars. Arrange the steaks and sear for 1 minute each side. Move the steaks to a cooler part of the barbecue and continue cooking over a moderate heat or turn the heat down. If the heat can't be reduced, elevate the steaks on a wire cakerack placed on the broiler bars. Cook 5–6 minutes for rare, 7–10 minutes for medium and 10–14 minutes for well done. Turn during cooking.

3 To make garlic butter, mix all ingredients together

4 Serve the remaining garlic butter in a small pot with a spoon.

Serves 4

Chicken Satay Skewers

Preparation 1 hr 15 mins **Cooking** 20 mins **Calories** 295

500g (18oz) chicken thigh fillets

Satay Sauce Marinade
½ cup peanut butter
½ cup water
1 clove garlic, crushed
1 tbsp brown sugar
pinch chili powder or to taste
2 tsps soy sauce
1 tbsp shredded onion

1 Mix all the satay sauce ingredients together in a saucepan. Simmer and stir occasionally for 5 minutes. Allow to cool completely.

2 Soak bamboo skewers in water. Cut the thigh fillets into cubes, place in a bowl and mix in the cooled satay sauce. Cover and stand to marinate for 1 hour or longer if refrigerated.

3 Thread 4–5 cubes onto each skewer, spaced to be almost touching. Heat the broiler or barbecue to medium high and cover with a sheet of baking paper. Place the skewers on the paper and cook for 12–15 minutes, turning and brushing frequently with the remaining satay sauce. Increase the heat for the last 3–5 minutes to brown and cook through. Serve immediately.

Serves 4

Note: For party finger food, thread 3 cubes onto small skewers. Small skewers may also be pan broiled.

Lebanese Lamb Rolls

Preparation 20 mins **Cooking** 20 mins **Calories** 165

2 tbsps oil

1 onion, chopped

500g (18oz) ground lamb

1 small eggplant, cubed

2 tsps ground allspice

1 tsp chili sauce

3 tbsps red wine

440g (1lb) canned tomatoes, undrained and mashed

4 tbsps sultanas

3 tbsps pine nuts, toasted

4 large pita bread rounds

4 lettuce leaves, shredded

1 carrot, peeled and shredded

1 Preheat the oven to 180°C (350°F). Heat oil in a large skillet and cook onion for 3–4 minutes or until softened. Add lamb and cook over a medium–high heat for 5 minutes longer or until brown. Stir in eggplant, allspice, chili sauce, wine, tomatoes and sultanas. Bring to the boil, then reduce heat and simmer for 5 minutes, or until sauce has reduced and thickened slightly. Stir in pine nuts.

2 Heat pita breads in the oven for 5 minutes or until heated through but not crisp. Spread with lamb mixture, top with lettuce and carrot, and roll up. Serve immediately.

Serves 4

Marinated Grilled Fish with Basil Tomato Topping

Preparation 2 hrs 10 mins **Cooking** 4 mins **Calories** 125

4 x 200g (7oz) white fish fillets

Marinade
1 tbsp shredded onion
2 tbsps olive oil
2 tbsps lemon juice
¼ tsp ground black pepper
½ tsp salt or pepper, to taste
3 bay leaves

Topping
10 basil leaves
2 tomatoes, sliced
1 tbsp shredded Parmesan cheese

1 Place the fish in a single layer in a non-metallic dish. Mix together the marinade ingredients and pour over the fish. Cover and marinate for 2 hours in the refrigerator.

2 Remove the fish from the marinade. Preheat the broiler, cover with baking paper and place the fish on top. Close the broiler and cook for 3 minutes or according to thickness, until the fish just flakes. Open the broiler, place 3 basil leaves on top. Cover with 2–3 slices of tomato and top the tomato with cheese. Cover with a sheet of baking paper, close the lid and cook for 30–40 seconds. Remove immediately to heated plates and serve with desired accompaniments.

Serves 3–4

Monkfish and Prosciutto with Braised Capsicums

Preparation 10 mins **Cooking** 25 mins **Calories** 303

3 tbsps extra virgin olive oil

4 large red, green, orange, or yellow capsicums deseeded and thickly sliced

4 cloves garlic, chopped

2 sprigs fresh thyme

salt and black pepper

4 monkfish fillets, about 225g (9oz) each

4 slices prosciutto

2 tbsps balsamic vinegar

chopped basil leaves to garnish

1 Heat 2 tablespoons of the oil in a large heavy-based saucepan, then add the capsicums, garlic, thyme, 2 tablespoons of water and the seasoning. Cook, partially covered, for 20 minutes or until softened and browned, stirring occasionally.

2 Meanwhile, season the monkfish well, then wrap a slice of prosciutto around each fillet. Secure the prosciutto with a wetted cocktail stick. Heat the remaining oil in a large heavy-based skillet, add the fillets and fry for 8–10 minutes, turning once, until browned and cooked through. Cover loosely with aluminum foil and set aside.

3 Add the vinegar to the capsicums in the pan and cook for 5 minutes to warm through. Remove the cocktail stalks from the monkfish and prosciutto, then cut the monkfish into thick slices and garnish with the basil. Serve with the capsicums and pan juices.

Serves 4

Note: Delicately flavored monkfish wrapped in prosciutto is a wonderfully luxurious combination. For a really pretty dish, choose different-colored capsicums.

Grilled Tuna in Vegetables

Preparation 12 mins **Cooking** 5 mins **Calories** 125

3 tbsps olive oil

2 tbsps balsamic or red-wine vinegar

1 tbsp chopped basil leaves

freshly ground black pepper

4 baby eggplants, halved

4 plum tomatoes, halved

1 leek, cut into 7½cm (3in) pieces and halved

4 tuna steaks

1 Place oil, vinegar, basil and black pepper to taste in a bowl and beat to combine. Brush eggplant, tomatoes, leek and tuna with the vinegar mixture.

2 Heat a lightly oiled skillet over a high heat, add vegetables and tuna and cook, brushing frequently with remaining vinegar mixture, for 2 minutes each side or until vegetables and tuna are cooked. To serve, arrange vegetables and tuna on serving plates and serve immediately.

Serves 4

Note: When cooking fresh tuna take care not to overcook it. The experts recommend that you cook tuna so that it is still pink inside. If tuna is unavailable this recipe can also be made using swordfish or salmon.

Parmesan-Crusted Fish

Preparation 25 mins **Cooking** 10 mins **Calories** 345

4 firm white fish fillets
½ cup flour
1 tsp paprika
freshly ground pepper
1 cup dried breadcrumbs
90g (3oz) shredded Parmesan cheese
1 egg, lightly beaten
2 tbsps olive oil

Lemon Thyme Butter
60g (2oz) butter
1 tbsp grated lemon rind
1 tbsp stet lemon juice
1 tbsp chopped fresh thyme or lemon thyme

1 Pat fish dry. Combine flour, paprika and black pepper to taste. Combine breadcrumbs and Parmesan cheese. Coat fillets with flour mixture. Dip in egg, then coat with breadcrumb mixture. Heat oil in a skillet over a medium heat, add fillets and cook for 2–3 minutes each side or until cooked.

2 To make the lemon thyme butter, heat butter, lemon rind, lemon juice and thyme in a saucepan over a medium heat for 1 minute or until butter melts. Serve with fish fillets.

Serves 4

Serving suggestion: Accompany with potato chips and vegetables. Make the chips using a vegetable peeler and peeling thin slices from potatoes. Dry slices and deep-fry for 7–10 minutes or until cooked. Drain and sprinkle with salt.

Note: When buying fish fillets, look for those that are shiny and firm with a pleasant sea smell. Avoid fillets that are dull, soft, discolored or 'ooze' water when touched.

Shellfish and Arugula Pizzas

Preparation 10 mins **Cooking** 15 mins **Calories** 635

24 whole jumbo shrimps, defrosted if frozen

2 tbsp olive oil

2 cloves garlic, crushed

12 small prepared squid tubes, cut into rings

2 x 23cm pizza bases

2 tbsp sun-dried tomato purée

16 anchovy fillets in oil, drained and chopped

1¾ cups mozzarella cheese, shredded

½ cup arugula

Parmesan cheese to serve (optional)

1   Preheat the oven to 220°C (425°F). Put 2 large baking trays into the oven to heat.

2   Rinse the shrimp and pat dry with absorbent paper. Heat the oil in a large heavy-based skillet, add the garlic, shrimp and squid and stir-fry for 3 minutes, or until the shrimp turn pink and the squid is opaque.

3   Spread the pizza bases with the tomato purée and top with the cooked seafood, anchovies and mozzarella. Place on the heated baking trays and cook for 10–12 minutes, until the cheese is golden, swapping shelves halfway through. Scatter the arugula over the pizzas and shave over the Parmesan (if using) with a vegetable peeler.

Serves 4

Note: Anyone who likes good food will love this shellfish and arugula pizza. If you're cooking for 2, halve the quantities and reduce the cooking time by a couple of minutes.

Gratin of Scallops and Mushrooms

Preparation 10 mins **Cooking** 10 mins **Calories** 175

4 large fresh scallops

145ml milk

145ml (5fl oz) heavy cream

30g (1oz) flour

30g butter

¼ tsp freshly shredded nutmeg

55g (2oz) Gruyère or Lancashire cheese, diced

115g (4oz) button mushrooms trimmed and halved

2 tbsps butter, extra

1 Trim the scallops, remove the orange coral and cut the white flesh of each scallop into 8 pieces.

2 Pour the milk into a non-stick saucepan. Add the scallops (except for the corals), bring to the boil and simmer for 5 minutes. Remove the scallops from the milk and set aside.

3 Add the cream, flour, butter, and nutmeg to the milk and beat gently over a low heat until the sauce thickens. Add the cheese and allow to melt without letting it boil.

4 Sauté mushrooms in the extra butter for 2–3 minutes.

5 Spoon some scallops onto the center of each serving plate. Arrange mushrooms around the scallops. Drizzle any juices over the mushrooms.

6 Top scallop pieces with corals and cover with the sauce.

Serves 4

Swordfish with Cilantro Butter

Preparation 6 mins **Cooking** 10 mins **Calories** 423

½ cup unsalted butter

2 tbsps finely chopped cilantro leaves

1 tbsp shredded Parmesan cheese

4 swordfish steaks

1 tbsp olive oil

4 zucchinis, cut into long slices

1 red capsicum, quartered

1 Cream the butter until soft and mix in the cilantro and Parmesan. Pile into a butter pot and set aside.

2 Heat the barbecue or broiler until hot and brush with oil. Brush the fish steaks with oil and cook for 3–4 minutes each side according to thickness. Brush or spray vegetables with oil and cook for a few minutes on each side. Remove the fish steaks and vegetables to heated plates. Top each swordfish steak with a generous spoonful of the cilantro butter and serve immediately.

Serves 4

Salmon with Pineapple Salsa

Preparation 6 mins **Cooking** 10 mins **Calories** 344

4 salmon chops

Pineapple Salsa

1 cup canned crushed pineapple, drained

2 scallions, chopped

1 fresh red chili, chopped

1 tbsp lemon juice

2 tbsps chopped mint leaves

1 Cook the salmon on a lightly oiled preheated barbecue or under a broiler for 3–5 minutes each side (or until cooked).

2 To make the salsa, combine all the ingredients. Serve with the salmon.

Serves 4

Variation: Exchange the pineapple for 1 cup fresh diced mango.

Seafood and Noodle Stir-fry

Preparation 20 mins **Cooking** 5 mins **Calories** 464

2 tbsps sesame oil

1 clove garlic, crushed

2 small red chilies, chopped

1 tbsp grated fresh ginger

900g (1lb) prepared mixed seafood

½ red capsicum, sliced

½ cup snowpeas, cut into 2cm pieces

225g (9oz) asparagus spears, cut into 2.5cm (1in) pieces

1 tbsp shredded basil leaves

340g (12oz) egg noodles, cooked

1 tbsp cornstarch

¼ cup hoisin sauce

½ cup water

2 tbsps sesame seeds, toasted

1 Heat the oil in a wok. Add the garlic, chili and ginger. Stir-fry for 1 minute. Add the seafood, capsicum, snowpeas, asparagus and basil. Stir-fry until the seafood is just cooked. Add the noodles. Stir-fry for 1–2 minutes.

2 Combine the cornstarch, hoisin sauce and water. Stir into the pan. Cook, stirring, until the sauce boils and thickens. Sprinkle with the sesame seeds and serve.

Serves 4

Asparagus and Lemon Risotto

Preparation 15 mins **Cooking** 25 mins **Calories** 363

2 tbsps olive oil

1 onion, chopped

2 cups arborio rice

1 cup white wine

3 cups chicken or vegetable stock

1 cup asparagus tips, cut into bite-sized pieces

4 tbsps butter

½ cup Parmesan cheese, shredded

salt and black pepper

2 tbsps chopped fresh parsley

finely grated zest of 1 lemon

1 Heat the oil in a large, heavy-based saucepan or skillet, then add the onion and fry for 3–4 minutes, until golden. Add the rice and stir for 1 minute or until coated with the oil. Stir in the wine and bring to the boil, then reduce the heat and continue stirring for 4–5 minutes, until the wine has been absorbed by the rice.

2 Pour about a third of the stock into the rice and simmer for 4–5 minutes, stirring constantly. Once the stock has been absorbed, add half the remaining stock and cook, stirring, until absorbed. Add the remaining stock and the asparagus and cook, stirring, for 5 minutes or until the rice and asparagus are tender but still firm to the bite.

3 Add the butter and half the Parmesan and season. Cook for 1 minute, or until the butter and cheese have melted into the rice, stirring constantly. Sprinkle with the remaining Parmesan and the parsley and lemon zest.

Serves 6

Note: Rich, creamy, and full of flavor, this fabulous risotto is very easy to make. Be sure not to overcook it; each grain of rice should keep its shape and firmness.

Asparagus, Ricotta and Herb Frittata

Preparation 10 mins **Cooking** 20 mins **Calories** 430

455g (1lb) fresh asparagus

12 medium eggs

2 small cloves garlic, crushed

4 tbsps chopped fresh mixed herbs, including basil, chives and parsley

salt and black pepper

4 tbsps butter

100g (4oz) ricotta cheese

squeeze of lemon juice

olive or truffle oil to drizzle

Parmesan cheese to serve

fresh chives to garnish

1 Preheat the broiler to high. Place the asparagus in a broiler pan and broil for 10 minutes or until charred and tender, turning once. Keep warm.

2 Meanwhile, beat together the eggs, garlic, herbs and seasoning. Melt 2 tablespoons of the butter in an ovenproof skillet until it starts to foam, then immediately pour in a quarter of the egg mixture and cook for 1–2 minutes until almost set.

3 Place under the preheated broiler for 3–4 minutes, until the egg is cooked through and the top of the frittata is set, then transfer to a plate. Keep warm while you make the 3 remaining frittatas, adding more butter when necessary.

4 Arrange a quarter of the asparagus and a quarter of the ricotta over each frittata, squeeze over the lemon juice, season and drizzle with oil. Top with shavings of the Parmesan, garnish with the fresh chives and serve.

Serves 4

Note: Grill the asparagus brings extra texture and flavor to this Italian-style frittata and the creamy ricotta adds the finishing touch. Serve with warmed crusty ciabatta.

Variation: Exchange the ricotta for feta cheese.

Roman Kebabs

Preparation 10 mins **Cooking** 8 mins **Calories** 597

1 French baguette
455g (1lb) mozzarella cheese
4 tomatoes
5 tbsps olive oil
1 tbsp lemon juice
1 tsp dried oregano
salt and black pepper
fresh basil to garnish

1 Preheat the oven to 230°C (450°F). Soak 4 bamboo skewers in water for 10 minutes.

2 Cut the bread into 16 1cm (⅓in)-thick slices, and cut the mozzarella into 12 slices. Slice each tomato into 3, discarding the ends.

3 Combine the oil, lemon juice, oregano and seasoning in a shallow dish. Generously brush both sides of the bread with the oil, then thread the bread onto the skewers, alternating with the mozzarella and tomato slices and finishing with bread. Pour over any of the remaining oil mixture.

4 Place the kebabs on a baking sheet and cook for 6–8 minutes, carefully turning over halfway through, until the bread is crisp and the cheese is just starting to melt. Cool slightly before serving and garnish with the fresh basil.

Serves 4

Spinach, Olive and Feta Frittata

Preparation 15 mins **Cooking** 25 mins **Calories** 616

10 eggs, lightly beaten
1 tbsp fresh oregano, chopped
freshly ground black pepper
5 tbsps olive oil
225g (9oz) potatoes, peeled and diced
1 onion, diced
1 clove garlic, crushed
2 cups baby spinach
4 tbsps black olives, pitted and halved
½ cup feta cheese, crumbled
½ cup semi-dried tomatoes
3 large red capsicums

1 Combine the eggs and oregano in a bowl, season with black pepper and set aside.

2 Heat the oil in a 23cm (9in) pan and sauté the potatoes, onion and garlic for a few minutes until soft.

3 Add the spinach and cook until it begins to wilt. Remove the pan from the heat, then add the olives, feta and semi-dried tomatoes.

4 Return the pan to a very low heat, pour in the egg mixture and cook for 10–15 minutes. Run a spatula around the sides of the pan as the frittata is cooking and tilt it slightly so that the egg mixture runs down the sides a little.

5 Meanwhile make the capsicum sauce. Halve the capsicums and remove the seeds. Chargrill the capsicums until black under a broiler. Let them cool and remove the skins. Place into a blender and process until puréed. Transfer to a bowl. Makes 1 cup.

6 When the frittata is almost done through the middle, place it under a broiler for 5 minutes to cook and brown the top.

7 Serve in wedges with the roasted capsicum sauce.

Serves 4

Feta and Ricotta Stuffed Tomatoes

Preparation 5 mins **Cooking** 25 mins **Calories** 198

6 large firm tomatoes

1 cup feta cheese, crumbed

1 cup ricotta cheese

4 tbsps pine nuts, chopped

10 black olives, pitted and chopped

1½ tbsps fresh oregano, chopped

3 tbsps whole-wheat breadcrumbs

freshly ground black pepper

6 black olives, to garnish

oregano leaves

1 Preheat the oven to 180°C (350°F). Cut the top quarters off each tomato and scoop the centers into a bowl. Reserve the tops of the tomatoes. Combine half the tomato mixture with the feta, ricotta, pine nuts, olives, oregano, breadcrumbs and pepper. Beat the mixture together and spoon it back into the tomato cases (piling the tops high). Replace the tops on each tomato.

2 Place in a shallow ovenproof dish and bake for 20–25 minutes.

3 Garnish with an olive and the oregano to serve.

Serves 6

Deep-Fried Okra

Preparation 8 mins **Cooking** 2 mins **Calories** 283

225g (9oz) okra
1 egg
1 cup flour
1 cup ice-cold water
oil, for frying

Garlic Walnut Sauce
2 slices bread
½ cup water
½ cup walnuts
2 cloves garlic, roughly chopped
2 tbsps white-wine vinegar
1 tbsp olive oil
salt and black pepper to taste

1 To make the garlic walnut sauce, soak the bread in water for 5 minutes. Squeeze out the water. Place the walnuts in a blender, and process until finely chopped. Add the bread, garlic and vinegar. Process until combined. While the motor is running, add the olive oil, salt and pepper and process until a paste is formed.

2 Wash and trim the okra. In a large bowl, beat the egg until frothy, add the flour and water and beat together until the batter is also frothy.

3 Heat the oil in a large skillet, dip the okra in the batter and cook in the oil for 1–2 minutes or until lightly brown.

4 Drain on absorbent paper and serve with the lemon wedges and the garlic walnut sauce.

Serves 4

Note: The garlic walnut sauce goes equally well with chicken, fish or vegetables.

Eggplant Rolls

Preparation 8 mins **Cooking** 25 mins **Calories** 384

2 eggplants (about 225g (9oz) each)

3 tbsps olive oil

3 medium tomatoes, seeded and diced

1 cup mozzarella cheese, finely diced

2 tbsps basil leaves, chopped

salt and freshly ground black pepper

extra basil leaves, for serving

Dressing

4 tbsps olive oil

1 tomato, diced

1 tbsp balsamic vinegar

2 tbsps pine nuts, toasted

salt and black pepper

1 Remove the stalks from the eggplants and slice them lengthwise in 5mm (⅕in) sections. Brush the slices on both sides with oil and grill both sides until soft and beginning to brown.

2 Preheat the oven to 180°C (350°F). In a bowl, combine together the tomatoes, mozzarella, basil and seasoning. Spoon a little onto the end of each slice of eggplant and roll up. Place it seam-side down in a greased ovenproof dish and bake for 15–17 minutes.

3 Meanwhile, make the dressing/olive oil in a small pan, using a little of the dressing oil, sauté the tomato until softened. Add the remaining oil, vinegar and pine nuts, and gently warm through. Season to taste. Arrange the eggplant rolls on a platter and spoon the dressing over them.

4 Garnish with the fresh basil leaves.

Serves 4

Mini Chocolate Muffins with Mocha Sauce

Preparation 15 mins **Cooking** 15 mins **Calories** 160

4 tbsps butter, diced, plus extra for greasing

½ cup semisweet chocolate, broken into pieces

2 medium eggs

⅓ cup superfine sugar

¾ cup flour

¼ tsp baking powder

⅕ cup cocoa powder, sifted, plus extra for dusting

Mocha Sauce

1 cup semisweet chocolate, broken into pieces

⅓ cup espresso or other strong, good-quality coffee

⅝ cup double cream

1 Preheat the oven to 180°C (350°F). Grease a 12-hole muffin tray. Melt the butter and chocolate in a bowl set over a saucepan of simmering water. Combine the eggs, sugar, flour, baking powder and cocoa powder into a bowl and beat for
1 minute, then beat in the melted chocolate and butter.

2 Spoon into the muffin tray, allowing 1 tablespoon for each hole. Bake for 15 minutes or until risen and firm to the touch.

3 Meanwhile, make the mocha sauce. Put the chocolate, coffee and a quarter of a cup of the cream into a small pan and heat gently. Simmer for 1–2 minutes, until the sauce has thickened slightly. Keep warm.

4 Leave the muffins to cool on a wire rack for 5 minutes. Beat the remaining cream until thickened, then spoon over the muffins together with the mocha sauce. Serve dusted with the cocoa powder.

Makes 12

Note: You'll need a 12-hole, non-stick muffin tray for these mini muffins or, if you prefer, you can make large muffins and increase the cooking time to 25 minutes.

Raspberry and Elderflower Fool

Preparation 45 mins **Calories** 371

3 cups raspberries, defrosted if frozen, plus extra to decorate

4 tbsps elderflower cordial

4 tbsps confectioner's sugar, or to taste, plus extra to dust

2 cups heavy cream

fresh mint to decorate

1 Purée the raspberries and cordial until smooth in a blender. Blend in the icing sugar. Spoon 1 tablespoon of the mixture into each dessert glass, reserving the remaining purée, and set aside.

2 Beat the cream until it holds its shape, then gradually fold into the reserved raspberry purée.

3 Spoon the raspberry cream into the glasses and chill in the fridge for 30 minutes. Serve decorated with the extra raspberries and mint and dusted with the confectioner's sugar.

Serves 6

Note: A fresh-tasting fruit fool that needs no cooking. Other fruits, such as strawberries or blackberries, can be used, but you may need to adjust the quantity of confectioner's sugar.

Sweet Brioche with Grilled Peaches

Preparation 10 mins **Cooking** 12 mins **Calories** 420

4 large, ripe peaches, halved and stoned

1 tbsp clear honey

6 tbsps unsalted butter

2 medium eggs, lightly beaten

2 tbsps sweet white wine

2 tbsps superfine sugar

1 tbsp lemon juice

pinch of ground cinnamon

4 slices brioche

crème fraîche to serve

1 Preheat the broiler to medium. Place the peach halves, cut-side up, in a broiler pan and top each with a drizzle of honey and a knob of butter, reserving half the butter for frying. Broil for 5–6 minutes, until softened and golden.

2 Meanwhile, beat together the eggs, wine, sugar, lemon juice and cinnamon. Dip the slices of brioche in the egg mixture to coat.

3 Melt the remaining butter in a large skillet and gently fry the brioche slices for 2–3 minutes each side, until crisp and golden. Top each slice with 2 peach halves and their juice and a spoonful of crème fraîche.

Serves 4

Note: Don't worry if the peach stones won't come out easily. Simply cut the fruit away from the stone in thick juicy slices and broil them for slightly less time than for halves.

Variation: Use 2 croissants, halved, instead of the brioche.

Flourless Chocolate Cake

Preparation 10 mins **Cooking** 45 mins **Calories** 188

6 eggs, separated
½ cup superfine sugar
⅕ cup cocoa powder, sifted
1 cup bittersweet chocolate, melted

Toffee
½ cup superfine sugar

1 Preheat the oven to 180°C (350°F). Beat the egg yolks with the sugar until thick and creamy. Mix in the cocoa powder and chocolate. Beat the egg whites until soft peaks form. Fold into the chocolate mixture. Pour into a greased and lined 23cm (9in) springform pan. Bake for 35 minutes. Cool.

2 To make the toffee, melt the sugar in a heavy saucepan over high heat. Shake the saucepan so sugar browns evenly. Bring to a boil and cook until golden. Pour onto a sheet of greased aluminum foil and allow to set. Break into large pieces and use to decorate chocolate cake.

Serves 12–14

Index